Cont

Act One, Scene One	1
Act One, Scene Two	7
Act One, Scene Three	14
Act Two, Scene One	20
Act Two, Scene Two	24
Act Two, Scene Three	29
General Vision and Viewpoint	36
Cultural Context	39
Literary Genre	43
Relationships	46

CLASSROOM QUESTIONS • 1

Act One, Scene One

Summary

This scene takes place in a graveyard as Maggie Polpin buries her husband, Walter. She is glad that he has died and tells her children that big changes are about to be made in their lives, with her in charge.

The play opens in a graveyard. Walter Polpin, Maggie's husband, is being buried. Maggie smokes, dressed in black, while an Old Man and Old Woman pay her their respects.

When the elderly couple leave, Maggie refuses to lay wreaths, saying she does not want to look at the graveside mourners pretending to be sorry.

Maggie tells her daughter Gert to stay with her, saying that the wreaths will not do her husband any good now. Maggie has a poor opinion of him and does not want to be a hypocrite.

Maggie asks Byrne, the ornamental sculptor, to begin work on the headstone straight away, rather than waiting the customary three months. She haggles with Byrne, paying him £60 cash there and then.

She refuses Byrne's suggestions of adding to her proposed inscription, saying she does not want to lie on the headstone.

Gert says that Maggie could not have hated Walter so much and wonders what will happen next. Maggie intends to call a family meeting. Maggie does not like it when Gert asks about money and she slaps her when Gert is cheeky.

Maggie's sons Maurice and Mick and her daughter Katie arrive. Maggie accuses Katie of overdoing her tears and challenges her sons for never defending her from their father. She warns her children that big changes are on the way.

Maurice is embarrassed by the way the family are conducting themselves publicly. Maggie says they must go and open the shop, to Katie's disbelief.

Teddy Heelin arrives and offers his condolences. He gives Maggie and Gert a lift to town.

The Old Man, Old Woman and Byrne talk about Maggie. Byrne says she is comfortable financially. He says that Maggie and her husband were a bad match. Byrne says that Walter was not the worst of them when the Old Man and Old Woman mention that they heard he was fond of women and whiskey.

Byrne says he has known all sorts of men given to womanising and suggests that it is all part of God's design. He directs the old couple to Madge Gibbons' grave and the scene closes.

Points to Consider

Students may be taken aback by Maggie's undisguised hatred of her husband and her refusal to pay her respects at his graveside.

It is worth noting how the backstory of this relationship is introduced - the audience receives a lot of information about Maggie's marriage from Byrne and the elderly couple, rather than from Maggie herself. This is worth discussing, as it tells a lot about their small rural community.

The Polpin family appear to be very dysfunctional and discordant. This is interesting to discuss, considering they are at their father's/husband's funeral. It is worth speculating what may have made them this way, as it helps students to become involved in the story and engage with the play.

It can be interesting to discuss what sort of man Walter Polpin was. Maggie appears as a force to be reckoned with, yet she says that her husband abused her. Consider what this suggests about him, and their relationship.

Note the references to religion, money and death in this opening scene and how these references help to build the audience's perceptions of the story that is unfolding.

Maggie's attitude to the headstone reveals a lot about her character. She conducts her business in a no nonsense, direct way and does not care about what others might say or think. She does not mourn her husband, she refuses to conform or behave as she is expected to.

Questions

1. Describe the scene as the play begins.

2. What information do you learn about Maggie's husband from the Old Man and Old Woman?

3. Is Maggie interested in talking to the Old Man and the Old Woman?
   What makes you say this?

4. How does Maggie's behaviour change when the elderly couple leave?

5. Why does Maggie refuse to lay on the wreaths?

6. What are your first impressions of Maggie?

7. What are your first impressions of Gert?

8. Describe Maggie's attitude towards her dead husband.

9. What does Maggie want Byrne to do for her?
   How much does she pay him?
   What is your reaction to Maggie negotiating the price with him there in the graveyard?

10. What does Maggie refuse to include on her husband's headstone?
    What does this suggest about her relationship with her husband?

11. What does Maggie's comment about the direction the headstone will face reveal to you about her marriage?

12. Comment on the way Maggie treats her daughter, Gert, in this opening scene.

13. How does Maggie react when Gert stands up to her? What does this tell you about Maggie?

14. How does Maggie react to Katie's arrival?

15. Maggie is angry with her sons. How does she accuse them of letting her down?
    Why has she chosen to address them now?
    Is she being entirely fair to them?

16. What does it mean, to 'blackguard' someone?

17. What impression are you forming of Maggie's dead husband? Support the points you make with suitable quotation.

18. What impression are you forming of the Polpin family? Support the points you make with suitable quotation.

19. Maggie tells her children that she intends to make changes they might not like.
    Describe the atmosphere at this point.

20. Why is Katie alarmed that Maggie plans to open the shop?

21. What opinion do the Polpin brothers have of Teddy Heelin?

22. Does Katie have a similar view?

23. The Old Woman says that Maggie is a dab hand at breaking spirits. Does this comment about Maggie surprise you?

24. What information does Byrne's conversation with the elderly couple provide about Maggie's marriage and financial situation?

25. "Still, you must admit now that he sired a noble share of likely men."
    What does the Old Man mean here?
    What is your reaction to this?
    How does this comment contribute to the picture you are forming of Walter Polpin?

26. How does Byrne explain Walter's womanising?
    Does he consider adultery to be a serious offence, do you think?

27. Why couldn't the old couple find Madge Gibbons' grave? Does this tell you anything about the world of the play?

28. How do Byrne's words at the end of the scene add to it? Explain your answer.

… CLASSROOM QUESTIONS • 7

Act One, Scene Two

Summary

Maggie is a controlling, dominant figure. Her children are annoyed that they will not receive anything as a result of their father's death. Maggie denies Maurice his request to marry, as the girl has no money. Maggie refuses to give Mick a share of the farm, so he leaves. Maggie forces Katie to accept a marriage proposal from a man she is not interested in. She knows Katie had sex with a married man and wants to save her reputation.

This scene takes place in the Polpin shop as Maggie tells her children of the changes that are to come.

Maggie tells them that there is no will, that everything has been signed over to her. They are annoyed that they are not getting what they perceive as their share of their father's fortune.

Mick demands half of the farm, but gets no support from his brother Maurice, who has had his fill of arguing for one day.

Maurice says that he would like to get married, but Maggie dismisses the proposed match unless the girl can come up with a dowry of £1,500.

When Maggie goes to answer the door, Katie tells Maurice and Gert that their mother caught their father in bed with Moll Sonders a year ago. She thinks this explains why Walter signed the place over to Maggie.

Maggie tells Gert that she will work in the shop in future, while Katie works in the kitchen, a swap that infuriates Katie.

Mick returns, wanting money from the cashbox, seeing it as his due. He threatens Maggie and takes the money. She tells him never to return if he leaves with the money. He goes.

Maggie sends Gert out to the kitchen. Maggie tells Katie to accept a marriage proposal made to her a year ago by Johnny Conlon. Katie laughs.

Then Maggie starts questioning Katie about the creamery social, a dance she attended. Maggie knows that Katie spent two and a quarter hours in the hotel room of Toss Melch, a married man. Katie is afraid here, as Maggie asks her questions.

Katie denies doing anything wrong, but she does not convince her mother. Maggie slaps and shakes her until Katie admits to committing a sin with the man. Katie is very upset and shook up.

Maggie tells Katie to write back to Johnny Conlon and she agrees to.

Points to Consider

Note how self-centred and money focused characters are.

Maggie scoffs at Maurice's desire to get married. She is very dismissive of his wish to marry and treats him like a child.

Katie interprets Walter signing everything over to Maggie as the result of him being caught in bed with another woman, Moll Sonders.

Interestingly, Katie does not condemn her father's actions here. While Maurice and Gert are shocked to hear Katie remark that their mother didn't sleep with their father, Katie has no problem openly discussing her parents' sex life.

Maggie's suggestion that Katie could make a living as a prostitute will provoke a reaction from students. Some will feel that Maggie is unkind and rude to say such a thing about her own daughter, while others may admire Maggie's spirit and may find it amusing rather than outrageous.

Note the way the family members threaten each other with violence if they do not get their own way. Are they bullies? Consider how these threats create an atmosphere and help build the audience's view of this world.

Questions

1. Where does this scene take place?

2. What is on Mick's mind?

3. Maggie tells her daughter, Katie, that she trusts no-one. What is your response to this?
   What sort of outlook is this to have?

4. Does Maggie treat her children well?

5. How does Maggie explain the lack of a will?
   Do you believe her? Explain your answer.

6. What conclusion does Katie jump to when Maggie says everything has been signed over to her?
   What does this tell you about Maggie's character?
   What does it tell you about her relationship with Katie?

7. What does Mick demand from his mother?
   Why doesn't Maurice back Mick up here?

8. Does Maggie appreciate Maurice's support?
   What is your response to this?

9. What does Maurice want to do?
   How does Maggie react?
   What is your response to this?

CLASSROOM QUESTIONS • 11

10. Maggie says she would like Mary Madden, Maurice's intended, a lot better if she had £1,500. Comment on the way Maggie treats her son here.
Is Maggie mocking her son?
Is this part amusing or not? Explain your view.

11. Does Maggie take her son's wish to marry seriously?

12. Do you feel sorry for Maurice?

13. What does Maggie's treatment of Maurice suggest about her character?

14. What does her treatment of Maurice suggest about Maggie's attitude to love and marriage?

15. Does Maggie care about what her children want?

16. Is Maggie a very hard mother, in your view?

17. Why do the others resent Katie?

18. What happened a year ago with Moll Sonders?
What is your reaction to this?
What does this have to do with Walter's will?

19. What differing views of their father do Katie and Gert have?

20. How does Maggie speak to Katie in this scene?
What is your reaction to the way she treats her daughter?

21. Where does Maggie want each of her daughters to work? Why is this problematic?

22. What insulting remark does Maggie make about Katie? What does this tell you about Maggie? What does it tell you about her attitude to her daughter?

23. Why does Mick return?

24. Are you shocked by Mick's behaviour here?

25. What ultimatum does Maggie give Mick?

26. Maggie accuses her family of causing her trouble in this scene. Is Maggie bringing these problems on herself, or are her children to blame?

27. How does Maggie try to control Katie in this scene? What demand does Maggie make of Katie regarding Johnny Conlon? What is your reaction to this?

28. What does Maggie interrogate Katie about once she has her alone? What is your response to this story? What is your response to the way Maggie treats Katie?

29. Why does Maggie slap Katie?

30. What does Katie admit to? Why is this such a big deal? What does this tell you about their society?

31. What are your impressions of Maggie and her children at this point in the story?

32. Is there a lot of tension in this scene? Explain, using examples.

33. Are you surprised that Katie seems broken by Maggie as this scene ends? Explain your view.

Act One, Scene Three

Summary

Gert plans a date with Teddy. However, Maggie warns Teddy to keep away from Gert and arranges to meet him herself.

The scene opens in the Polpin shop, with Gert serving Byrne.

Teddy comes in and learns from Byrne that Katie has married. Teddy is surprised that she has settled down. He jokes with Byrne, making innuendoes about Katie.

Gert is delighted to see Teddy. She asks him when he is going to ask her out, saying that Maggie won't mind. Teddy says he will take her out that night. Gert warns Teddy not to get fresh with her, saying she is not the type. He responds by saying that he knows this about her and that it is what he likes about her. They flirt and kiss briefly.

Byrne returns and Gert remarks to Teddy that she thinks he is after her mother.

Maggie comes in and sends Gert to the kitchen. She tells Teddy to keep away from Gert and they speak openly about his interest in her. Maggie says it comes down to sex, while Teddy says it is something more.

Their conversation moves from Gert to relationships. They are interested in seeing each other and plan to meet that night.

Points to Consider

Note the sexist, derogatory way that Teddy speaks with Byrne about Katie. It is similar in language and tone to the way Byrne spoke about Walter in the graveyard.

Teddy's reason for not asking Gert out before now is Maggie. Consider the tight control Maggie wields over her daughters and the way she limits their freedom.

Gert suspects that Byrne has an interest in Maggie. This is worth considering in light of Maggie's conversation with Teddy.

Students tend to react strongly to the way Maggie's chat with Teddy quickly moves on from a discussion of Teddy and Gert to that of Maggie and Teddy. Her actions here are often viewed as a cruel betrayal.

Teddy's conversation with Gert was suggestive, but innocent and flirtatious. This can be contrasted with the blunt, direct conversation about sex he has with Maggie.

Maggie is knowingly and wilfully blocking Gert from seeing Teddy, making plans to sleep with him herself. Maggie does not care about the heartache her actions will cause Gert. Both her approach and the hurt she is causing her daughter are worth discussing.

The age difference between Maggie and Teddy is worth mentioning and can be interesting to discuss.

Questions

1. Are you surprised that Gert is working in the shop?

2. What news does Byrne have about Katie?
   What does this tell you about life since Walter died?

3. "And how do you know I didn't score a few bullseyes there before this?"
   What does Teddy's remark about Katie mean?
   What is your reaction to the way he speaks about her here?
   Do his remarks here tell you anything about his character?

4. How does Gert respond to seeing Teddy in the shop?
   Why does she act this way?

5. Is Gert forward in the way she speaks to Teddy? Explain your view.

6. Is Teddy afraid of Maggie? Quote to support your answer.

7. Are you surprised to hear that Maggie lets Gert out now?

8. Gert warns Teddy not to get fresh with her, saying she's not that kind.
   What does this mean?
   What does this tell you about the way women are viewed and treated in this text?

9. Teddy tells Gert that he knows she's not the type to get fresh with, saying this is why he wants to go out with

her.
Is Teddy being honest here, do you think?
Why does he say this to Gert?

10. Teddy says he just wants to be near Gert. Is he trying to charm her here or is he sincere?
Do you expect Gert to fall for this?

11. Describe the conversation between Gert and Teddy in the shop.

12. Are you surprised that Gert kisses Teddy?

13. Gert suspects that Byrne has a romantic interest in Maggie.
Do you agree with her?

14. What information do we learn about Katie's husband?

15. Describe Maggie's appearance when she arrives in the shop.
Does her appearance tell you anything about how she has been since her husband died?

16. What does Maggie say to Teddy about Gert?
Why does she do this?

17. What does Teddy tell Maggie about his interest in Gert?
Do you believe him?

18. Are you surprised that Maggie and Teddy talk so openly about sex?

19. Maggie and Teddy begin discussing Gert, but what turn does their conversation take?
What is your reaction to this?
Are you surprised to find they have an interest in one another?
Can you explain this development?

20. Comment on Maggie's date with Teddy.
How is Maggie treating Gert here?

Act Two, Scene One

Summary

Maggie's tryst with Teddy is a set-up, for Gert's benefit. Maggie arranged the whole thing so that Gert would witness Teddy's real character.

Byrne calls to the shop to propose to Maggie, but she insults and refuses him.

Teddy arrives and he and Maggie embrace and kiss each other. Gert returns and sees them together. She realises she has been set up to discover them and leaves in a rage.

Teddy tells Maggie that she should not have done this, that she was cruel and has shamed him, but Maggie does not care. She feels she has taught Gert a valuable lesson.

Points to Consider

Maggie has set Teddy up, to show Gert the kind of man he is.

Some students will think she is very cruel, others may be relieved that Maggie is not really after Teddy herself. Her motivation and behaviour here make for interesting discussion.

It is worth considering how we judge Maggie when we think she is 'stealing' Teddy from Gert, and how quickly this changes once we realise her real intentions.

Also, it is worth considering whether Maggie has actually done Gert a favour by exposing Teddy.

Questions

1. What is life like for Maurice, based on his conversation with Byrne?

2. What advice does Byrne have for Maurice?
   What does this mean?

3. How does Maggie speak to Byrne?

4. What does Byrne say to Maggie to try to win her over?
   What do you make of this proposal?
   How does Maggie respond?
   What makes Maggie free to refuse Byrne?

5. How does he react to being refused?

6. Why is Maggie interested in Teddy, do you think?

7. What is your reaction to Gert's return?

8. "I had no idea you would stoop to do a thing like this."
   What has Maggie done?
   Are you shocked by Maggie's behaviour?

9. Why did she set Teddy up like this?

10. Does Maggie care about Gert?

11. How does Teddy react?

12. Does Maggie have any sympathy for Teddy? Do you? Explain your standpoint.

13. Do you understand Maggie's reasons for acting this way?

14. What judgements did you make about Maggie when you thought she was after Teddy?
Why did John B. Keane manipulate us like this?

Act Two, Scene Two

Summary

Katie speaks to Maggie on Maurice's behalf, attempting to convince Maggie to let him marry. Maggie is unmoved, even when Maurice arrives to talk about the matter himself.

Katie is paying Maggie for groceries as the scene opens. The pair jibe at each other while they talk.

Gert has left. She is living with Mick in England and doing nursing. Katie asks what happened the night Gert left and Maggie says it was the beginning of Gert's education.

Katie advises Maggie to let Maurice marry the Madden girl, but Maggie is unmoved.

Katie then suggests that Maggie take on a girl to help her with her work, but Maggie refuses.

Byrne comes in and Maggie encourages him to give some money to Katie's child. He repeats his offer to Maggie, but she is not interested.

The Old Man and Old Woman from the graveyard come into the shop to buy sugar. Maggie is very rude to them, in contrast to Katie who chats about Mick and Gert.

Katie tells Maggie she has come to talk about Maurice, but Maggie is not interested in his plight.

Maurice comes in and explains to his mother that he has run out of patience and wants to marry, despite her suggestions that he wait another year.

He says that he will go to England if Maggie won't allow him to marry Mary Madden. Maggie stands firm, but tries to convince him not to go. He leaves.

Katie points out to Maggie that she will be left all alone. Maggie says she can always marry Byrne.

Points to Consider

Maggie believes that she did Gert a favour by showing Teddy up for what he really is. Even though Gert won't speak to her, Maggie is certain she did the right thing and is glad to hear that Gert is doing nursing in England. It is worth discussing whether students feel sorry for Maggie here, or if they feel she has brought Gert's anger on herself.

Katie seems quite happy with her lot in life. Following her mother's instructions and marrying has not led to unhappiness, something worth noting and discussing.

Leaving for England is the only escape route for Maggie's children. There is something sad in the way she pushes them away in her attempts to toughen and protect them.

Questions

1. How are Maggie and Katie getting along as the scene opens?

2. What do we learn about Gert?

3. Why has Maggie not heard from Gert?
   What does this tell you about their relationship?

4. Does Maggie think she was right to treat Gert as she did? Explain Maggie's point of view.

5. What does Katie advise Maggie regarding Maurice?

6. Why does Katie encourage Maggie to take on a girl to help her?

7. How does Maggie respond to the Old Woman's request for a pound of sugar?
   What does this tell you about Maggie?
   What other details support this view of her?

8. What view does Maggie have of the old couple?

9. What is your reaction to Byrne's repeated offer of marriage here?
   Why does he want to marry Maggie, do you think?

10. Is Katie happy with how her life is turning out?
    Use examples to support your view.
    Is there a lesson in this for the audience?

11. Why has Katie come to see Maggie?

12. Do you think Maurice's wish to marry now is unreasonable?

13. What will Maurice do if Maggie does not permit him to marry?

14. Does Maggie care that Maurice is in love?
    What is your response to this?
    What does this tell you about Maggie's outlook?

15. What insulting comments does Maggie make about Mary Madden?
    What is your reaction to this?

16. Is Maggie treating Maurice fairly here?
    What would you do, in his position?

17. Does Maggie seem concerned that each of her children has left her?

18. Does Maggie care about her children, in your view?
    Why does she treat them like this?

Act Two, Scene Three

Summary

Maggie has a showdown with Maurice and the Maddens in this final scene. Mary is pregnant but Maggie does not see this as something that concerns her. Maggie refuses to allow Maurice to marry Mary, holding firm even though she realises it will cost her her relationship with her son.

The play closes with a monologue, where Maggie blames the church for forcing her to suppress her urges and feelings. She vows to live what remains of her life freely.

The scene begins with Maggie on the phone, chasing up a debt.

Mary Madden comes in to speak to Maggie. She is shy, explaining that her mother and Maurice made her come.

Maggie accurately guesses that Mary is pregnant. She is glad that she didn't sign anything over to Maurice, remarking that she would be badly off if she had. She accuses Mary of being out to land a comfortable position for herself and her siblings at Maggie's expense.

Mary gets annoyed with Maggie, but getting nowhere, changes tack and speaks respectfully towards her. Maggie however, is not moved.

Mrs Madden and Maurice come in. Mrs Madden is belligerent, demanding that Maggie do something for her daughter, a demand that Maggie refuses, even when Mrs Madden threatens a boycott of the shop.

Maggie advises Maurice to break with Mary now, before it is too late. He is upset and angry, feeling he is being forced to England with nothing, by his own mother.

Mary tells Maggie that she will make sure that Maurice never comes to see her in the years ahead. She says that she will make him stop Maggie's other children from coming too.

Mary leaves and Maggie is left alone onstage. She speaks openly, blaming the church for choking the love and lust in her. She remembers a man, Martin, who she desired but never pursued. She resolves to use what remains of her life to savour who and what she can and sleep with a man if he should take her fancy.

Points to Consider

Maggie is glad that she didn't sign anything over to Maurice as he requested. Maggie sees Mary Madden as a schemer who is after her wealth. She revels in the clever way she protects herself financially, seeming not to care that her behaviour will cost her her relationship with her son.

Some students will say Maggie is bitter and will dismiss her desire to protect her estate. However, it is worth considering whether Maggie is in fact a shrewd businesswoman, who has the measure of Mary Madden.

Maggie's advice to Maurice to break with Mary now may annoy students as Maggie refuses to consider what her son wants. However, the audience has to consider whether Maggie believes that leaving Mary would be best for him. Her advice seems cold, but it may spring from genuine care and affection.

It is interesting that Maggie is unconcerned about Mary Madden's pregnancy. She feels no obligation to provide for Mary or her own grandchild, nor does she seem concerned about Maurice's reputation. It is worthwhile to consider her outlook here and what it tells us about Maggie as a character.

Students often feel sorry for Maggie after her final speech. They may pity her because of the way her life has been stifled by religion, feeling that she has become cold and hard because of her circumstances.

Some may feel that she genuinely wants the best for her children, but that her lack of warmth has robbed her of a loving relationship with her family.

By the end of the play, Maggie is no longer a wife, or mother in a sense, as she has pushed her children away. By casting off the roles assigned to her because of her gender, she is free to pursue her business career and a sexual relationship of her choosing. She is alone, though not necessarily doomed to unhappiness as the play closes.

Her final resolve and forward-looking stance may be considered hopeful and optimistic in the face of poor personal relationships.

Questions

1. What does Maggie's conversation with Whacker Flynn reveal about her business affairs?
   What does it reveal about her character?
   Do you think Maggie enjoys chasing up debts? Explain your answer.

2. Who comes to see Maggie?
   Why has she come?
   How does Maggie react to this visitor?

3. What are your first impressions of Mary Madden?

4. What does Maggie guess about Mary?
   Are you surprised that Maggie knew this?
   How does Maggie react to this news?

5. What does Maggie accuse Mary of being after?
   Do you think Maggie is right to be suspicious, or do you think that Mary truly loves Maurice? Explain your view.

6. Mary changes her approach with Maggie.
   What makes her do this?
   Does this reveal anything to you about Mary's character?

7. Mrs Madden asks Maggie what she intends to do about Mary.
   What is going on here?
   Is Mary Madden's pregnancy Maggie's problem?

8. What sort of woman is Mrs Madden?

9. How does Mrs Madden threaten Maggie?
   How does Maggie respond to her threats?

10. What does Maggie advise Maurice to do?
    Does this advice surprise you?

11. How does Maurice react to his mother's conversation with Mrs Madden?
    Do you feel sorry for Maurice here?

12. Mrs Madden says Maggie is as hard as nails.
    Is Maggie a hard woman, in your view?

13. What does Mary promise Maggie before she leaves?
    How do you react to this?
    Do you blame Mary for behaving this way?

14. What does Maggie's monologue at the end of the play reveal about her?

15. What was Maggie's marriage like for her?
    What is your response to this insight?

16. Who dominated Maggie's sex life, morals and thoughts?
    What point is the playwright making here?

17. Does Maggie blame herself for her husband's affairs?
    Explain your view.

18. What does Maggie hold responsible for robbing her life of love and joy?
    Do you think this comment is fair?

CLASSROOM QUESTIONS • 35

19. Who was Martin?
    What does this recollection reveal about Maggie and her life?

20. What does Maggie resolve to do with her remaining years?
    What is your response to this?

21. Why has John B. Keane included this personal insight into Maggie's life at the end?

22. Is this a happy or sad ending, or something in between? Explain your view.

23. Do you feel sorry for Maggie Polpin as the play ends?
    If you could give her any advice, what would it be?

General Vision and Viewpoint

General Vision and Viewpoint refers to the author's outlook or view of life and how this viewpoint is represented in the text.

1. The play opens in a graveyard.
   How does this help to establish the mood?

2. What does Maggie haggling over the price of a headstone in the graveyard suggest about her attitude towards her dead husband?

3. In Act One, Scene One, Mick says that their house was never a home.
   What picture of this family are you forming?
   Is it a positive or negative impression?
   What sort of life do you think they have had?

4. What sort of life has Maggie had?
   How does this contribute to the General Vision and Viewpoint of this section?

5. How do the Old Man and Old Woman add to the mood of the opening scene? Explain your point of view.

6. In the scene following the graveyard, Maggie's children are fixated on the issue of their father's will. What does this tell you about their outlook and priorities?

CLASSROOM QUESTIONS • 37

7. How do Walter Polpin's affairs and womanising contribute to the mood of the play?

8. How do the threats of violence the family members make to one another affect the atmosphere of the story?

9. Katie bows to her mother's will and marries accordingly. What does this relationship suggest about life?
What does Katie's lack of freedom to make decisions for herself suggest about life? Will she be happy? How does this make you feel?

10. Maggie views Mary Madden as a scheming gold-digger, she does not consider that Mary may love Maurice. Comment on this view of life.
What does it suggest about happiness?

11. Maggie runs her own shop and enjoys financial independence as a widow. Does this bring her happiness?

12. How do you respond to the dominance and power Maggie wields over her children?
Is this a comforting or disturbing portrayal of a family?

13. In the long term, Maggie will be alone as she pushes her children away. Does this create a bleak outlook for her future?

14. What does his play suggest about human nature?
Is the outlook positive or negative?

15. Is there a lesson or moral to this story?
    What could it be?
    Does it still hold true today?

16. There is a sense of loss in Maggie's final speech.
    How does this shape the General Vision and Viewpoint of the text?
    Is there any hope in her outlook as the play ends?

Cultural Context

Cultural Context refers to the world of the text.
Consider social norms, beliefs, values and attitudes.

1. Maggie slaps Gert in the graveyard.
   What does this reveal about this world?

2. In the opening scene, Maurice is concerned by how the family are acting.
   What does Maurice mean here?
   What does this tell you about their world?

3. What rumours are there about Walter Polpin?
   Do these rumours tell you anything about this world?

4. What attitude does Byrne have towards Walter's womanising?
   What does this tell you about this world?

5. Do these characters strike you as being very religious?
   Use examples to support your view.

6. What is the significance of Walter not having a will?
   What are Maggie's children concerned about?
   What does this suggest about their values?

7. What does the focus on the will, ownership of the farm and Mary Madden's dowry, tell you about this society and characters' values?

8. What does Maggie's knowledge of her husband's womanising suggest about this world?

9. In Act One, Scene Two, Katie suggests that women in this world have little interest in sex. What reason does she give for this? What does this suggest about their marriages? What does this suggest about their lives?

10. Is this a violent world? Use examples to support the points you make.

11. Katie has disgraced herself as she was seen leaving the hotel room of a married man. What does this tell you about the world of the play?

12. In Act One, Scene Three, what do Teddy's remarks to Byrne about Katie reveal about his attitude to women?

13. Gert warns Teddy not to "get fresh" with her as she is "not that kind" and he assures her his intentions are good. Comment on what this reveals about these characters' values and their attitude towards sex.

14. Katie's husband is wealthy. Do you think this influenced her decision to marry him?

CLASSROOM QUESTIONS • 41

15. What conventions does Maggie break by pursuing Teddy? What other conventions does she break in the play? Does maintaining the status quo bring characters happiness in this world?

16. What does Byrne's proposal to Maggie reveal about the world of this text and how these people measure happiness and success?

17. Why is Maggie able to refuse Byrne? What gives her the ability to choose a man, if she cares to do so?

18. Maggie suggests that Mary Madden intended to use her pregnancy to trap Maurice and get hold of Maggie's shop and farm.
What does Maggie's attitude here tell you about her views towards love, marriage, family and wealth?

19. Mrs Madden thinks that Mary's pregnancy is Maggie's concern.
What does her attitude here reveal to you about the world of the play?
What is your response to her attitude here?

20. What does Maggie's marriage show you about the world of this text?

21. Who controlled her sex life, according to Maggie? What does this tell you about this world?

22. How significant a factor was the Church in Maggie's life? Was it a positive or negative influence, in her view? What does this suggest about this world?

23. What is the role of women in the world of this play?

24. Is the role of wife and mother a palace or a prison in this text? Is it both?

25. What does Maggie's final speech reveal to you about the Cultural Context of this play?

26. What comments does this play make about life in Ireland at this time?

Literary Genre

Literary Genre refers to the way the story is told. Consider aspects of narration such as the manner and style of narration, characterisation, setting, tension, literary techniques, etc.

1. What are your first impressions of Maggie?
   How is her character established in the opening scene?

2. How does the playwright develop her character?

3. Do you like Maggie?
   Is she an attractive or repellent protagonist?

4. How does John B. Keane establish tension in the opening scene?
   Where else does he make use of tension and suspense?
   How does this add to the story-telling?

5. How do the Old Man and Old Woman add to the opening scene?
   What does Byrne add?

6. How does the matter of Walter's will contibute to the story?

7. Is there humour in this play? If so, where?
   Does this add to the story?

8. How is tension built throughout Act One, Scene Two?
   Is this a very exciting scene?
   Does it involve the audience and draw them in well?

9. What draws the audience into this story?
   Clearly identify each element in your answer.

10. Identify the various sources of conflict in this text.
    How does the use of conflict add to the story?

11. How does the episode with Maggie and Teddy increase tension and further the plot?
    How does John B. Keane manipulate his audience?
    How does this add to the story?

12. How is tension built in the final scene?

13. What makes Maggie such an interesting lead character?

14. Why did John B. Keane choose to close the play with Maggie's confessional address to the audience?
    What is the effect of this?
    How does it complete the story?

15. Did you enjoy this story? Explain your answer, using examples from the text.

16. Who is your favouite character in this play?
    What makes you like/admire them?

17. Who is your least favourite character in this play? What makes you dislike them?

18. What themes can you identify in this story?

19. How does setting help tell the story of the play?

Relationships

The theme of relationships can be applied to any relationship in a text and includes love, marriage, friendship and family bonds. Consider the complexities of relationships and the impact they have on characters' lives.

1. How does Maggie treat Gert in the graveyard?

2. What does Maggie's conversation with Byrne about Walter's headstone tell you about her relationship with her husband?

3. What sort of marriage does Maggie seem to have had?

4. In Act One, Scene Two, Maggie and her children meet in the family's shop. What are they concerned about?
   Do they miss their father?
   Do they get on well?
   What does their conversation reveal about their relationships and how they view one another?

5. Maggie dismisses Maurice's wish to marry. Does this tell you anything about her relationship with her son?

6. Why does Maggie threaten to strike her children? What does this tell you about their relationships?

CLASSROOM QUESTIONS • 47

7. How does Maggie try to dominate and control each of her children?
   Is she successful?

8. Describe Gert's relationship with Teddy.
   Was Maggie cruel to set Teddy up?
   What does this tell you about Maggie's relationship with Gert?

9. Does Maggie love her children?
   Does she understand them?
   Does she communicate well with them?
   Do Maggie's children love and respect her?
   How do they feel about her?

10. Comment on the state of Maggie's relationships with her children as the play ends.

11. Are relationships in this story positive or negative?
    What makes them this way?

12. Are a lot of the relationships in this text characterised by conflict? Explain your point of view.

13. Comment on Maurice's relationship with Mary Madden.

14. Do relationships in this play bring characters happiness or sorrow? Include examples in your answer.

CLASSROOM QUESTIONS GUIDES

Books of questions, designed to save teachers time and lead to rewarding classroom experiences.

SCENE BY SCENE

www.SceneBySceneGuides.com